Original title:
Vines and Verses

Copyright © 2025 Creative Arts Management OÜ
All rights reserved.

Author: Nora Sinclair
ISBN HARDBACK: 978-1-80567-287-6
ISBN PAPERBACK: 978-1-80567-586-0

Music in the Garden of Shadows

In a garden of whispers, we dance with glee,
Where shadows jive and jump like a bee.
The daisies crack jokes, the roses all laugh,
While carrots and cabbages play a new half.

A tomato's a singer, with a voice so bold,
As cucumbers sway, with stories retold.
But the lettuce just sighs, with a leaf-edge frown,
Claiming he's seen all this go down.

The potatoes spin tales of their life in the dirt,
As radishes chuckle in comedic spurt.
They tap dance on roots, with a punchline so neat,
While the sunflowers sway to this fun little beat.

When shadows grow long, and the moon starts to peek,
The garden erupts in a chorus unique.
With nature's own band, we laugh 'til we cry,
In this quirky green space, under stars in the sky.

Twists of Earthly Inspiration

In a garden where gnomes like to dance,
Twirling round flowers, they take a chance.
One step too far, and down they flop,
Rolling on soil till the giggles stop.

With carrot sticks armed like tiny swords,
They battle the veggies in jovial hordes.
Under the sun, their antics so spry,
Laughter erupts as the radishes fly.

The Harmonies of Growth

Beneath the tomatoes, a salsa parade,
With onions and peppers, a grand charade.
They sway and they jiggle, like creatures in tune,
As the moon chuckles softly, 'What's coming, you croon?'

Each sprout tells a story, or so they believe,
Of romaine romances and the fate of a seed.
With a wink and a spin, they flirt with the sun,
'Join us, dear rain, for a party of fun!'

Blossoms Beneath the Canopy

Where daisies gossip and daisies plot,
The sunflowers wonder, 'Are we all that hot?'
Petals whisper secrets in soft silly tones,
While bumblebees groove on pollen-filled phones.

A dandelion's wish flies as it giggles,
Dodging the cat who jumps and wiggles.
'Catch me if you can,' it teases with flair,
As the breeze carries laughter all through the air.

Nature's Mesmeric Paragraphs

In the book of the garden, the chapters entwine,
With peas telling tales that are simply divine.
Each leaf turns a page with a dramatic flair,
While potatoes plot world domination with care.

With a plot twist involving some crafty old mud,
They conspire to paint the hard pan with crud.
With roots in a tangle, it's hard to keep straight,
But laughter grows wild, so who needs to wait?

Growth of Gentle Rhyme

In a garden of words, sprout they do,
Twisting like pretzels, a puzzling view.
Leaves whisper jokes, fluttering around,
Nature's humor leaps, it knows no bound.

A sunflower giggles, its face in the sun,
While daisies play tag, oh what fun!
The trees laugh in tickles, rustling their chairs,
As bees buzz in minstrel, weaving light airs.

Spirals of Nature's Song

A worm in a dance, on a spiral path,
Sings to the raindrops, inciting a laugh.
Grassy notes flutter, like kites in the breeze,
Composing a symphony, happy with ease.

The clouds wear mustaches, they float and they sway,
As the sun plays the trumpet, brightening the day.
With each twist and turn, life is a jest,
In nature's embrace, we find humor blessed.

Leaves that Speak

Oh, the leaves gossip, rustling with glee,
Telling tall tales of the old sycamore tree.
Each flutter's a chuckle, each spin's a grin,
As sunlight spills laughter, inviting us in.

Maples declare, "I'm the trendiest shade!"
While oaks bungle lines, their jokes don't quite trade.
In nature's great play, we find quirks galore,
With every flapping leaf, we giggle for sure.

Branches in Bloom

Branches in bloom, wear their best hats,
Fluffy like clouds, bantering like cats.
Each bud tells a story, with petals so bright,
While bumblebees chuckle, they dance in the light.

"Oh look!" says the twig, "I'm sprouting a friend!"
The flowers all cheer, "Let the fun never end!"
They sway to the music, of breeze's soft tune,
In this jovial orchard, laughter is strewn.

The Poetry Beneath Our Feet

In the garden, weeds compete,
With sonnets lost beneath our feet.
They wiggle, giggle, cheerfully shout,
A rhyming ruckus, no doubt.

Their roots twist tales, all entwined,
In dirt, funny fables are designed.
When we walk, they launch a jest,
A leafy laugh that never rests.

Each flower plays a part, you see,
In this chaotic comedy spree.
With petals bright, they roll in glee,
Like nature's own confetti spree.

So tiptoe lightly in this rhyme,
Join the dance, it's quite sublime.
For underfoot, a story flows,
Where humor blooms and laughter grows.

Gossamer Leaves and Lines

A leaf twirls down like a feathered friend,
Whispering jokes in the autumn bend.
It lands on my hat with a plop and a pop,
Who knew foliage could make such a stop?

The branches stretch their limbs so wide,
Hoping to catch a falling tide.
But instead of raindrops, they catch a sneeze,
Chasing the laughter of rustling trees.

Mossy tomes are piled high,
The library where the critters lie.
A squirrel reads loud, with acorn snacks,
As rabbits chuckle at metaphorical cracks.

Gossamer leaves dance in delight,
Spinning verses every night.
In the moonlight, they twinkle and tease,
Sharing secrets with the evening breeze.

The Quest of Spiraling Gardens

On a quest through twisted plots we roam,
In spirals that lead us so far from home.
With gnomes as guides and sunflowers tall,
Each turn we take, we start to sprawl.

Mice act out tales of great delight,
While ladybugs put on a show at night.
The lilies giggle at their own silly hats,
While frogs croak verses like old rhyming bats.

In this maze of humor, we trip and slide,
Through berry bushes, where laughter won't hide.
A tangle of blooms, so bright and bold,
Unraveling tales that never get old.

So join the quest, and do not despair,
For every garden has tales to share.
With a chuckle or two and a quip to pass,
In this spiraling journey, we're all bound to laugh.

Vibrations of Verdant Lyrics

In the jungle where the puns grow wild,
Every tree branches out, humor compiled.
The bushes hum with a rhythmic sway,
As nature sings, come join the fray.

The hedges whisper jokes in the breeze,
Tickling toes of unsuspecting knees.
With every rustle, a punchline's born,
In this green world, none can feel forlorn.

The soil chuckles, its earth-tone laugh,
As worms recite their scientific math.
The daisies clap under sunny beams,
Making music that sparks our dreams.

So dance with joy, oh merry crowd,
As the garden rocks, we laugh out loud.
In verdant lyrics, we find our cheer,
Nature's symphony, so crystal clear.

Climbing the Lines of Thought

In the garden of my mind, I tread,
With squiggly thoughts just like a thread.
Hopping thoughts like frogs on spring,
Wrestling logic, it's quite the fling.

Each idea dangles, ripe for the pick,
I reach for a nugget but trip on a stick.
Laughter echoes, what a grand mishap,
Climbing the lines with a silly cap.

A twist of fate, a slip of rhyme,
I find madness in the climb.
Twisting, turning, up and down,
Mental acrobat, I wear a crown.

So let the jests and giggles flow,
As I scale this wobbly show.
Each thought a berry, red and sweet,
In my mind's tangle, I can't be beat!

Blossoms of Reflection

Petals flutter like a funky hat,
As I ponder where I'm at.
Reflecting on my quirky ways,
In a mirror maze of silly days.

The blooms shout secrets that they keep,
Every laugh not far from sleep.
I spill my tea while deep in thought,
Life's a jest, or so I've sought.

Buds are bursting with quirky cheer,
Each giggle blooms, come draw near.
I write my dreams in colors bright,
In this garden of giggles, all feels right.

With every sip, a splash of fun,
In this orchard, I've just begun.
The blossoms giggle, oh what a sight,
In this patch of mirth, life feels light!

Canopies of Heartfelt Ink

Under this canopy, I laugh and glow,
With thoughts that flip and twirl in tow.
Ink spills laughter on the page,
Writing whims of the quirky sage.

Beneath the leaves, I scratch my head,
Scribbling tales of flowers fed.
Each line a vine, winding and wild,
Pulling at the heart of a giggly child.

The raindrops giggle on leafy tips,
As I ponder on my silly quips.
Every drop a drop of cheer,
In this ink-touched space, all is clear.

So pen in hand, I dance and swirl,
With heartfelt scribbles, give life a twirl.
In my leafy nook, I'm fully braced,
For every giggle, my heart's embraced!

The Swaying Poetry of Time

Tick-tock goes the silly clock,
With words that dance, we'll take stock.
Time is a jester, playful and sly,
As it winks at us passing by.

Moments sway like a playful breeze,
Tickling toes, oh what a tease!
Time's poetry unfolds like a vine,
Stretching laughter, how divine!

Each hour blooms with a cackle and giggle,
Absurd antics that always wiggle.
The past is a canvas, bright and bold,
Swaying stories like yarn that unfolds.

So let's dance in this merry spree,
With words that tumble and run free.
For in this sway of funny rhyme,
Life's a jest, so pass the thyme!

Shades of Leafy Dreams

In the garden where the weeds dance,
Chasing shadows, taking a chance.
Lettuce giggles, carrots play tag,
While potatoes roll in a soil bag.

Bees are buzzing, oh what a sight,
Sipping nectar, feeling quite bright.
A squashed bug sings, 'give me some shade!'
While flowers chuckle in a parade.

Frogs in tuxedos leap down the lane,
Trying to dodge the summer rain.
Oh, what a party under the sun,
Nature's humor, oh so much fun!

Grapevines whisper, "Let's have some wine!"
As the sun dips low, it's evening time.
A toast to greens, with a hearty cheer,
In this leafy realm, we have no fear.

Rhythms in the Underbrush

In the thicket where the critters play,
Every rustle leads the dance away.
Squirrels spin in a nutty trance,
While the rabbits plot a daring romance.

A worm winks, he's got the groove,
As the ladybugs bust a move.
Lizards snap their tiny jaws,
While the larks just pause, because...

A cheeky mouse steals the last crumb,
As the hedgehogs roll, oh what fun!
With a jumpy jig and a silly shuffle,
In the underbrush, they're all in a scuffle.

Dance, you plants, don't be shy!
With the sun above in the blue sky.
In this wild mix, no one gets hurt,
Except for thorns that may squirt dirt!

A Tangle of Starlight

Under the moon, where secrets hide,
The fireflies shimmer, a whimsical ride.
Whispers of stars in the night breeze,
Casting giggles among the trees.

A chubby owl hoots with delight,
While raccoons host a feast tonight.
They pass the snacks with a nimble flair,
And giggle as they spin in the air.

Tangled lights in a cosmic embrace,
Not a worry, just fun in space.
Twinkling laughter fills the dark,
Each soft chuckle igniting a spark.

A comet streaks with a zany grin,
As the night creatures all join in.
With starlit dreams and laughter bright,
They weave their magic until daylight.

Blooms of an Unwritten Yearning

In the meadow, the daisies conspire,
To reach the clouds and go a bit higher.
They giggle as they flirt with the breeze,
While the butterflies dance with such ease.

The tulips tease with colors so bold,
Painting the world with stories untold.
In vibrant hues, they laugh and sway,
As bumblebees buzz in a merry array.

A shy sunflower lifts her head,
As tiny ants hold a parade instead.
"Oh, the day was dull," she says with a pout,
But soon they all cheer, dancing about.

Petals drop like confetti, quite free,
In this garden of joy, let's just agree.
With laughter blooming in sunshine's light,
Every moment feels so very right.

Ink Slips Between Petals

The ink drips, oh what a sight,
As petals giggle with delight.
A quirky quill with jokes to tell,
Spills laughter where the flowers dwell.

In gardens where the sunlight beams,
The blooms conspire with silly dreams.
They whisper secrets in the breeze,
Tickling bees with rhymes like these.

Each bud's a book of puns so bright,
They bloom with laughter, pure delight.
A stanza here, a joke quite fine,
The blooms recite like Shakespeare's line.

So gather round and hold your breath,
For flowered wit defies all death.
With petals bright and ink so true,
They pen their pranks for me and you.

Dreaming in Tangled Growth

In tangled realms where dreams collide,
The greenwood jokes, a leafy guide.
With roots that trip and leaves that sway,
Each branch unveils a cheeky play.

The shrubs do dance, with glee they twirl,
While busy bugs hum songs that swirl.
A comedy of nature's best,
Plant antics outshine all the rest.

The daisies chuckle on their stalks,
While sleepy snails share silly talks.
In every shade where shadows play,
Laughter blooms, come what may.

So join the ruckus, take a seat,
In this green theater, life's a treat.
With tangled thoughts and wild delight,
The flora gigs beneath the night.

The Melody of Wildflowers

In fields where wild blooms sway and sing,
A symphony of colors takes wing.
Each daffodil strums the strings of cheer,
With melodies that tickle the ear.

The daisies dance, a waltz in the breeze,
While poppies tease with such playful ease.
Nature's orchestra, a riotous sound,
As laughter springs from the rich, warm ground.

With every rustle, a joke unfolds,
In fragrant pitches, the story's told.
A chorus line of hues so bright,
Sings funny tales in pure sunlight.

So let the petals set the tone,
In wildflower croons, we find our own.
Joyful notes in the summer air,
A silly saga beyond compare.

Secrets Beneath the Foliage

Beneath the leaves, a world obscured,
Whispers of folly, secrets assured.
The fronds conspire, plotting their schemes,
As roots exchange the wildest dreams.

A cunning fox, a wise old crow,
Trade puns that only plants would know.
A snail narrates, his tales a hit,
While blooms erupt in fits of wit.

The shadows laugh where sunlight fades,
In leafy caverns, the humor cascades.
With crickets chirping their own refrain,
The verdant depths host a comic gain.

So lift your gaze and take a peek,
For underneath, it's fun and sleek.
A tapestry of jests to find,
In every leaf, a punchline twined.

Dew-Drenched Confessions

In the morning light, they glow,
Little drops with tales to show.
Whispers hang on leafy arms,
Laughing at the sun's bright charms.

A snail slid by on fancy grounds,
Mumbling jokes in funny sounds.
As petals giggle, swaying free,
Nature's laughs, just wait and see!

Ants parade with tiny hats,
Dancing round like silly cats.
Spiders weave their threads of cheer,
Tickling plants from ear to ear.

With every dawn, the secrets spill,
In a world that loves to thrill.
Amidst the leaves, the laughter stirs,
Tales of life without the blurs.

The Brush of Nature's Quill

With strokes of green, the trees compose,
A funny tale that never slows.
Each branch a line, each leaf a rhyme,
Drawing sketches, one at a time.

Squirrels sketch with acorn tips,
As laughter tumbles from their lips.
The wind, it giggles through the pines,
Giving voice to nature's puns and signs.

Rabbits hop, with brushes bright,
Painting scenes in morning light.
Every blade of grass a jest,
In laughter's arms, they take their rest.

Through the canvas of the day,
Nature's humor finds its way.
With every brush of joy and thrill,
It's a masterpiece, a joyful will.

Stories on Twisted Stems

In the garden, tales unwind,
Twisted stalks with laughs entwined.
Each flower winks and softly sighs,
Sharing secrets, oh, what a prize!

Bees buzz by with stories sweet,
Spinning yarns on nimble feet.
As petals toss their heads in glee,
Nature's chatter, wild and free.

A crooked stem holds jokes untold,
A humorous world for young and old.
Butterflies dance with slender grace,
Whisking laughter in their chase.

With every twist, a giggle blooms,
Filling up the air with zooms.
In leafy halls where fun extends,
Life's a joke that never ends.

The Music of Climbing Children

Up the trees, the laughter soars,
As little ones unlock the doors.
They climb so high, like tales in flight,
With giggles echoing, pure delight.

Branches bend and sway with cheer,
While joyful shouts are all we hear.
A symphony of kicks and screams,
Where every climb fuels crazy dreams.

They swing from leaves, like vines in haste,
Creating melodies, none go to waste.
With every jump, a new refrain,
Their fun, like sunshine after rain.

With sticky hands and muddy shoes,
They scribble jokes, they cannot lose.
In nature's choir, they find their voice,
In laughter's arms, they all rejoice.

Nature's Lyrical Embrace

In the garden, plants do dance,
Twisting twirls, they take a chance.
With each twist, they giggle loud,
Whispering secrets, oh so proud.

Bumblebees wear tiny hats,
Telling tales of where they're at.
Butterflies in capes so bright,
Flutter by, oh what a sight!

Under leaves, they play a game,
Who can shout out the silliest name?
Dandelions share their dreams,
Tickling toes, or so it seems!

Nature laughs in every turn,
In every leaf, a lesson learned.
With jokes tucked in the roots below,
Who knew plants could steal the show?

Trails of Secret Stories

In the woods, the path unfolds,
Squeaky mushrooms share their gold.
Squirrels gossip from the trees,
Spreading tales with playful ease.

A gnome is caught with tiny snacks,
Hiding goodies in his packs.
Rabbits leap through brush so thick,
Cracking jokes and being quick.

The wind whirls tales of old,
Of mushrooms brave and flowers bold.
Every rustle sings a song,
Inviting all to sing along.

Through the trails, laughter flows,
As nature pranks, nobody knows.
A tale of whimsy, gently spun,
Each step reveals another pun!

Memory's Green Tapestry

In the park, the memories gleam,
A patchwork quilt, an endless dream.
Each leaf has stories to unfold,
Of laughter shared and treats untold.

Sitting slow on benches tight,
Birds holler back at morning light.
The wobbly trees sway and bend,
Helping old folks round the bend.

Frogs croak out the latest scoop,
While ants march in a little troop.
With every bounce, the heart's aglow,
Nature's humor, in full flow.

Snapshots stitched with a giddy thread,
Of clumsy falls and laughter spread.
In every thorn and petal bright,
Memory flourishes, pure delight.

Syllables in the Breeze

As the breeze begins to hum,
Words take flight, oh what fun!
Leaves twist in a merry sway,
Spinning tales of yesterday.

Chirping birds share giggly tunes,
While the flowers nod like loons.
Each flutter holds a silly jest,
Nature knows how to be the best!

A tumbleweed rolls by with grace,
Whispering secrets, a jovial chase.
The clouds above play hide and seek,
Each shape they form will make you squeak.

And so the day rolls on with cheer,
Every sound brings laughter near.
In every moment, light and free,
Nature's joy is the key, you see!

Flora's Hidden Narratives

In a garden where humor blooms,
Each flower wears its own costume.
The daisies gossip, oh so bright,
While tulips joke about height.

A dandelion sings with glee,
Laughing at the bumblebee.
Petunias snicker, petals aflame,
While roses play a teasing game.

A sunflower steals the show,
Twirling in a silly row.
With morning glory's tangled cheer,
The blossoms sway, no hint of fear.

Every leaf a story to tell,
In nature's circus, all is well.
Each twisted stem and playful sprout,
Where laughter hides, and joy breaks out.

The Poetry of Wild Green

In meadows where the breezes play,
Laughter dances in the day.
The clovers chuckle at the breeze,
While bushes sway with utmost ease.

A squirrel cracks a witty pun,
His acorn stash is never done.
The oaks are wise, they nod and grin,
As vines above the fun begin.

Moss blankets rocks with gentle care,
While ferns throw jokes, if you dare.
The laughter rings through rustling leaves,
As every plant a secret weaves.

Wild green tales, both sweet and zany,
Spread through the woods, joyous and grainy.
In this lively, leafy scene,
Nature rejoices, ever keen.

Intertwined Harmonics

A melody of leaf and vine,
Sings a tune that's quite divine.
The branches sway with rhythmic grace,
Creating laughter in this place.

Willows whisper in the breeze,
Tickling the cheek of passing bees.
Harmonies from the roots below,
Pull up the chuckles as they grow.

Cedar trees play calypso tunes,
While lilacs dance beneath the moons.
Each rustle sparkles with delight,
As foliage kicks up joy in flight.

Together they form a merry band,
A silly symphony so grand.
In this leafy concert, we find,
A nature's jest that's unconfined.

Whims of Woodland Whispers

In the woods where whispers flutter,
Frogs croak jokes; the squirrels stutter.
Every shadow holds its charm,
With ghostly giggles, nothing's harm.

A fox in jest prances around,
Poking fun at the trees abound.
Leaves rustle with a playful grin,
As mushrooms laugh, where do they spin?

The pines stand tall, their jokes refined,
While thickets share what's intertwined.
Every twig a dusty quip,
As nighttime falls, let humor slip.

The woods a playground full of jest,
Where each creature gives its best.
In this realm of whimsy and cheer,
Every whisper brings laughter near.

Cadence in the Canopy

In the treetops, squirrels prance,
Wearing acorns like a fancy pants.
A bird sings loudly, thinks it's grand,
But slips on a branch, falls in the sand.

A chattering monkey swings with flair,
Dancing to rhythms floating in air.
The leaves all giggle, rustle with glee,
Nature's joke book, a sight to see.

When raccoons start a midnight feast,
They argue over who can eat the least.
Berries fly, laughter fills the night,
A comedy show under the moonlight.

With blossoms that twist and tease the breeze,
A caterpillar dons its leafy sneeze.
In the canopy, hilarity thrives,
As nature's antics keep us alive.

Flourishing Stanzas of the Earth

In gardens where daisies tell a joke,
Butterflies giggle, all wearing a cloak.
A snail races with a confident stride,
But trips over laughter, what a funny ride!

Bees buzz with sarcasm, sipping on thyme,
While frogs recite their poetry in rhyme.
The grass tickles toes, a playful tease,
As bumblebees dance around the trees.

Worms dig deep, plotting their best line,
Arguing over who'll find the next vine.
With roots entwined, they shake their heads,
In the soil, comedy's what they spread.

Under the sky's wide canvas of cheer,
Nature's oddities are always near.
In this patch of folly and growth so sweet,
The earth's funny tales, can't be beat!

The Enchantment of Climbing Hearts

Two squirrels are plotting a sneaky raid,
On a picnic spread, oh what a charade!
With acorn hats and mischief in eyes,
They leap to the table in hilarious surprise.

A rabbit named Benny wears lettuce cool,
While dancing on grass like a furry fool.
He trips on a root, flips right in a spin,
And giggles to plants, asking where to begin.

In the ivy's embrace, all secrets they hold,
A hedgehog whispers nonsense, truth be told.
As blossoms erupt in colorful cheers,
Nature's merry riot brightens our years.

As grapes hang on tendrils, swaying about,
A butterfly mucks up, causing a rout.
With banter and laughter in nature's fair art,
Every heart in their climb beats wild with jesting heart.

Nature's Silken Sonnet

A spider spins webs of tales slick and neat,
While ants hold a banquet, oh what a treat!
They argue on flavors of crumbs they have found,
In this banquet of nature, laughter abounds.

The grasshoppers serenade with a joke,
As daisies burst out laughing, feeling bespoke.
With petals that dance in the breeze's embrace,
Even flowers can smile with the sun on their face.

Down by the stream, the frogs start to croon,
With a splash of the water, they sing out of tune.
A fish rolls its eyes, swims swiftly away,
As farcical antics brighten the day.

Each leaf tells a story, a giggle, a sigh,
In nature's own sonnet under the sky.
With wild laughter echoing, life's clever play,
In the world spun of humor, we frolic and sway.

Whispers of the Green Embrace

In the corner, plants will sway,
They gossip more than we all say.
A fern lifts a frond with a wink,
While snails hatch plots over the sink.

Lettuce jokes with the old lychee,
"You've got more wrinkles, can't you see?"
Bamboo chuckles, tall and spry,
As daisies giggle, 'Oh my, oh my!'

The sunlight tickles every leaf,
With shadows dancing, oh what a relief!
The cactus rolls its spiky eyes,
As ivy whispers tales of surprise.

So next you visit your leafy friend,
Just know their humor will never end!
For in their green, both tall and small,
They laugh and play, the best of all.

Nature's Tangled Sonnet

Twisting trunks and climbing blooms,
Nature's chaos fills the rooms.
Here's a rose that swears it's tough,
While daisies giggle, 'That's enough!'

The ivy quips, 'You think you're grand?'
While daisies roll on the flower stand.
With every gust, they laugh and sway,
In their own wild, flowery way.

The poppies shout, "Got jokes galore!"
While violets hum, always wanting more.
The daisies tease, 'Oh, such a fuss!'
While tulips blush, all colorful and cussed.

So gather 'round, you garden pals,
Where laughter grows, in leafy halls.
For every petal's a punchline here,
A world of joy wrapped up in cheer.

Tendrils of Emotion

There's a twisty tale in each long tendril,
As plants weave stories, oh so gentle.
The poison ivy makes a sly jest,
While carrots giggle, burying their zest.

The lilacs laugh at the lumbering trees,
'You'll topple one day, just wait and see!'
The ferns chime in, a whispering sound,
'You're all too heavy for this ground!'

And when the wind pipes up with glee,
The flowers dance as wild as can be.
They share their dreams of sun and rain,
With whispers that echo, laughter unchained.

So let's toast to greens, both silly and grand,
Where every sprout has a well-worn stand.
For under the sun, with thrills abound,
Nature's jesters are intricately wound.

Lyrical Canopy

In the trees, where squirrels joke,
Leaves chuckle softly, 'A kiss, a poke!'
They mumble rhymes in rustling tones,
As branches dance and shake their bones.

The woodpecker rolls with a comic flair,
Knocking on wood like a stand-up air.
While mushrooms giggle, all tucked in tight,
Spreading spores with sheer delight.

The breeze plays games with every twig,
Making green things smile, oh so big.
And when the sun peeks through the leaves,
The laughter of nature is sure to please.

For in this canopy, lush and bright,
Life throws jokes in the warm sunlight.
So join the fun among the trees,
Where laughter flutters with every breeze.

Murmurs of the Sylvan Realm

In the wood where whispers creep,
A squirrel stumbles, takes a leap.
A raccoon waddles, winks his eye,
He steals my sandwich on the sly.

The trees are giggling, swaying slow,
Their branches tickle, don't you know?
A rabbit rants about his hat,
Of polka dots and beats a cat.

Beneath a patch of shaded green,
The mushrooms gossip, off unseen.
A butterfly in stripes so bright,
Tripped on a leaf, what a sight!

The brook, it chuckles, bubbling fast,
While frogs recite their jokes unsurpassed.
The crickets join the merry fun,
In nature's play, we all have won.

The Dance of Flora and Words

In the meadow, daisies twirl,
With partner bees, they leap and whirl.
A daffodil trips on a stone,
With petals flying, makes it known.

The dandelions puff and boast,
Of windy days and summer toast.
A bumblebee, with quite a buzz,
In search of nectar, or was it fuzz?

Ladybugs wear their polka dots,
Throwing parties in secret spots.
The sunflowers wink in evening's glow,
As if they know what's set to show.

The pollen rings, a great parade,
Each flower dancing, none afraid.
They whirl in circles, sing with glee,
Nature's humor, wild and free.

Lines of Nature's Palette

With brushes made of grass and dew,
The petals paint a lively hue.
A tulip sneaks a checkered grin,
While painted ladybugs dive in.

The trees conspire with cheeky eyes,
As doves compose their alpine sighs.
Colors splatter with every breeze,
Nature's art is sure to please.

A raspberry bush hums with sass,
As berries wobble, forms a mass.
It shouts, "I'm ripening, take a bite!"
And steals the show in morning light.

Beyond the hills, a chameleon waits,
In jokes of colors, it celebrates.
With every hue, a laugh it sparks,
In nature's palette, joy embarks.

Harmonies of the Overgrown

In the wild where laughter grows,
A pathway strewn with willow bows.
The hedges hum a raucous tune,
As grasshoppers jump beneath the moon.

The daisies dance a jig so spry,
While shrubs gossip 'bout the sky.
Mushrooms join in, quite uninvited,
Wobbling weakly, laughter ignited.

A thistle plays a cheeky chord,
Poking fun, it won't be ignored.
The lark sings high, a sweet refrain,
As sunlight filters through the lane.

They weave a symphony of cheer,
With rustling leaves that all can hear.
In tangled roots, they spin and sway,
Creating music every day.

Rhapsody of Roots

In a garden where gnomes dance with glee,
A worm holds a concert, just wait and see.
The carrots tap shoes, the peas start to hum,
While the radishes giggle, it's quite the fun!

The daisies are rapping, the tulips all cheer,
While a snail DJ spins tunes with great flair.
Each beetroot's a dancer, with moves like a pro,
In this rooty rave, everybody's a glow!

But watch out for squirrels, they can get a bit wild,
They'll join in the fun, oh yes, quite the child.
With acorn confetti and nuts in their hair,
This garden party, oh, it'll make you stare!

So grab all your veggies, come join in the jest,
In the Rhapsody of Roots, you'll find no rest!
With laughter and cheer in this leafy delight,
Every garden needs humor; it's simply just right!

Fables Under the Canopy

Beneath a thick canopy where tall tales are spun,
A beetle tells stories of battles, oh fun!
A gossiping leaf whispers truths quite absurd,
While a wise old frog croaks the best of the word.

The mushrooms are nodding, they're tipsy on rain,
Reciting their poems again and again.
The lightning bugs flicker, they light up the night,
As the crickets all chirp with great comic delight.

A squirrel's grand tale of a daring escape,
Involves a lost acorn and a daredevil cape.
With giggles ensue when the tale takes a spin,
And everyone laughs, for the fun's found within.

So gather your friends under leafy embrace,
For stories and laughter find their rightful place.
In this whimsical world, where the fables are spun,
You'll learn that with humor, life's double the fun!

The Echoing Thicket

In the thicket so dense, where the laughter grows loud,
A crow tells a joke to a rather bemused crowd.
His punchlines are cheesy, they float through the air,
While the bushes all chuckle, without a single care.

A fox in a top hat recites silly rhymes,
His friends all roll over, they're having a fine time.
With each clever quip the trees start to sway,
It's a roguish affair in the thicket today!

The owls find it funny; they hoot in delight,
As the rabbits all snicker, it's quite a silly sight.
Leaves rustle with mirth as they join in the jest,
Making echoes of laughter that surely won't rest.

So venture on in, where the chuckles are bright,
In the Echoing Thicket, everything feels right.
With tales and tomfoolery, there's joy all around,
In this merry habitat, happiness is found!

Breath of Evergreen Whispers

In a realm of tall evergreens, whispers take flight,
A squirrel plays tricks under soft moonlight.
He tosses down acorns, with mischievous cheer,
As the trees giggle softly, letting out a sneer!

With pinecones for microphones, they sing out loud,
Their laughter like music, it swells through the crowd.
A chipmunk declares, in a voice full of glee,
"That last acorn prank was the best, don't you see?"

The winds join the fun, with a playful breeze,
Tickling the branches, giving all a tease.
When shadows start dancing, and giggles abound,
In this evergreen haven, pure joy can be found.

So come take a trip to this forest of cheer,
Where laughter is carried on whispers sincere.
In the Breath of Evergreen, you'll find a delight,
A world full of fun, beneath stars shining bright!

Garden of Rhythms

In patchwork greens, the beans do swing,
They dance and giggle, it's quite a thing.
The peppers gossip, the carrots tease,
All while the chives play tag with the breeze.

A squash rolls by, it's full of cheer,
Whispering secrets for all to hear.
Tomatoes laugh, all plump and red,
While lettuce takes a nap in its bed.

Radishes plot a silly prank,
As flowers strut in their colorful rank.
With ferns as judges, they grant grand praise,
To the best dancer, in the sunny rays.

The bugs hold court, with crowns made of dew,
Dreaming up mischief in the garden's view.
A chorus of blooms in a playful tune,
The garden's alive, all dancing by noon.

Botanicals in Bloom

The daisies chuckle, their petals so fine,
They wink at the bees, sipping sweet wine.
Pansies prance in their polka dot dress,
While the daisies debate who's the best at chess.

Roses boast of their fragrant flair,
While daisies whisper, 'Life's hardly fair!'
The tulips gossip, in colors so bright,
Painting the garden in sheer delight.

But oh, the sunflowers, tall and spry,
Recounting tales as the clouds drift by.
They claim to be tallest, a real sensation,
The garden's comedians, a floral creation!

Beneath the moon, the petals will sway,
As crickets serenade the closing day.
With giggles and murmurs, the garden's a tune,
A merriment echoed beneath the moon.

The Song of Twisting Paths

Down twisted trails where herbs conspire,
Leeks and thyme hum with playful choir.
Mint teases basil, 'I'm cooler than you!'
While radishes blush in the leafy view.

The path is a twist, where fables ignite,
With partners of green in the glorious light.
They giggle through gardens, with carefree spin,
As roots tell stories of where they have been.

But oh, the garlic, a pungent prankster!
Whispers of mischief flow without transfer.
Carrots tease onions, all in good jest,
It's nature's gala, a gleeful fest!

From seedlings to harvest, in steps all aglow,
The tune of the earth sets a quirky show.
As paths intertwine in a colorful dance,
Life is a jest, in this garden's expanse.

Echoes Beneath the Arbor

Under the arbor, the squirrels convene,
Squabbling over acorns, it's quite the scene.
The vines overhead weave tales of delight,
As the shadows grow long with the fall of the night.

Chickadees chirp in a playful debate,
Who gets the best seat? They can't seem to wait.
Crickets join in, their rhythm profound,
Creating a symphony, a joy all around.

The breeze carries laughter, a sweet serenade,
As butterflies flutter, both bright and arrayed.
Here lies a banquet of whimsical cheer,
With every rustle, adventures draw near.

The plants hum along, a botanical choir,
Their secrets exchanged on the air like a fire.
Beneath the sweet boughs, the day takes its last,
And echoes of laughter in shadows are cast.

The Script of the Sylvan

In the woods there's chatter, quite absurd,
Trees gossip secrets, that haven't been heard.
A squirrel in glasses reads a fine text,
Critiquing the leaves, it's quite the perplex.

The mushrooms are dancing, in polka they go,
With a hedgehog DJ, putting on a show.
The flowers are snickering, petals a-flutter,
While the air's filled with laughter, a sweet, funny clutter.

The bushes form clusters, sharing their tales,
Of spiders' wild dreams and their grand epic fails.
Each twig has a story, a twist, and a turn,
In this scripted forest, there's so much to learn.

As sunlight drips down like syrup from trees,
The creatures unite to party with ease.
In this woodland theater, joy's in full swing,
With scripts from the sylvan, let the laughter ring!

Empires of Green Imagery

In a kingdom of leaves, where the sarcasm grows,
The cacti are jesters, with prickles like prose.
Lettuce debates with the broccoli heads,
Sharing their dreams of adventurous spreads.

Emerald castles, with peas on the wall,
Where carrots in armor prepare for the brawl.
Peas plan a coup, of this I'm quite sure,
While radishes bristle at rulers of yore.

In this realm of the verdant, each sprout wears a grin,
As the chives plot mischief, a playful new din.
The lettuce lords laugh from their leafy high thrones,
While spinach spins yarns of mystical zones.

As laughter does echo through the gardens so wide,
With bees as the chorus, buzzing with pride.
A banquet of folly, in a realm bright and keen,
In empires of green, where humor is seen!

The Whispers of Budding Stories

Underneath tangled branches, tales softly unfold,
Where snails are the authors, if truth's to be told.
With shells full of wisdom, they write, slow and wise,
Each slip 'n' slide chapter brings giggles and sighs.

Petunias discuss their grand role in the play,
While daisies do gossip, in a flowery way.
Overturning the soil, butterflies cheer,
As this bustling garden draws near the good cheer.

In the shadows, the thorns are plotting a plot,
While dandelions dream of a space they forgot.
The wrinkled old rhubarb shares tales of old,
With humor so sharp, in a language so bold.

So listen intently, to the whispers around,
For this garden of stories has magic profound.
In each little bud, and twist on the stem,
Are the tales of the garden, a laughter-filled gem!

Rhapsody of the Untamed

Amidst wildflowers growing, a rhapsody grows,
Where daisies do dance to the tunes of the toes.
The foxglove's a diva, in petals of lace,
Sings high and melodramatic, claiming her space.

The thistles debate on who's prickliest best,
As the daisies laugh, outshining the rest.
Bumblebees buzz with a comic reprise,
In this untamed theater, laughter's the prize.

Under the sun, where giggles ignite,
The grasses are tickled in morning's soft light.
With frogs as the audience, croaking in tune,
This rhapsody sways 'neath the bright, laughing moon.

So join in the revel, let your spirit roam,
In the wilds, find humor — there's plenty of room.
In the chaos of growth, and the fun of the chase,
The rhapsody's laughter finds its warm embrace!

Spirals of Time and Terrain

In a garden where gnomes like to lounge,
A raccoon in a hat starts to scrounge.
He steals all the carrots, the turnips too,
Leaving only a spinach for you to chew.

The daisies debate if they're flowers or weeds,
As the earthworms plot their mischievous deeds.
A scarecrow tells jokes to crows on a wire,
But the punchlines fall flat, which they all admire.

When the sun takes a nap, the moon makes a plan,
To dance with the stars, and forget about man.
But the wind plays a trick, swirls up the leaves,
And they tumble around like they're caught in a sneeze.

So let's laugh at the soil, and giggle at roots,
As earth chuckles softly in whimsical suits.
For time bends and twists in this playful domain,
Where laughter and dirt share the same crazy vein.

The Untold Narratives of the Wild

A squirrel in a cap tells tales of delight,
While his friends all nod, and applaud with great might.
They banter 'bout acorns buried with pride,
As a lizard swings by, in a fashion so wide.

The trees gossip softly about wandering feet,
Whispers of rabbits with musky retreats.
With giggles from foxes, and snickers from hens,
The forest is buzzing with chatter from friends.

A badger who bakes at the edge of a glen,
Keeps mistaking raw honey for various men.
The bees have declared it a scandalous error,
While hedgehogs roll on, in hysterics of terror.

So raise up your glasses, and crunch on some moss,
For the wilderness stories can be quite the gloss.
In this world of mischief, under sun's gentle smile,
Nature's the joker, who cracks jokes all the while.

Whispers in the Canopy

High above the ground where the monkeys swing low,
The parrot gossips in colors aglow.
He shares all the gossip of critters below,
As shadows intertwine in an acrobatic show.

A chameleon whispers secrets unheard,
While swinging like ribbons, a dazzling bird.
She's changing her hues like she's in a race,
As the monkeys just chuckle and roll 'round the place.

When the sun takes its bow behind leafy green,
And critters engage in their nightly routine,
The owls crack up jokes that they think are quite wise,
But the bats simply laugh as they swoop past the skies.

So listen close friends, to the tales of the trees,
Where laughter can float on the whimsical breeze.
In the canopy's dance, where the funny still thrives,
Each moment is vibrant, as nature alive.

Shadows of Twisting Blooms

In the patch of a garden, where daisies bloom bright,
The tulips conspire 'gainst the roses tonight.
With petals like fans, they flounce and they flirt,
While the sunflowers gawk, radioing dirt.

An old bumblebee brags of the pollen he's nabbed,
While the ants roll their eyes, for he's terribly drab.
The lavender chuckles at fragrances old,
As the marigold whispers daring and bold.

The shadows grow longer as the dusk settles in,
With fireflies buzzing, the night's bound to begin.
The blooms gather round with their silken chit-chat,
Sharing stories of bugs and mishaps and that.

So let's twirl in the twilight, with petals and cheer,
For the garden is lively, and laughter draws near.
In the shadows of flowers, where stories entwine,
The humor of nature is truly divine.

A Palette of Natural Stanzas

In a garden where giggles bloom,
Laughter dances, chasing gloom.
The flowers hum a quirky tune,
Bees wear hats, or so I assume.

Spilling paint with each new sprout,
Colors tumble, twist about.
The daisies argue, 'Who's more bright?'
While sunflowers grin, soaking light.

Petals gather, forming cliques,
Telling tales, pulling tricks.
A flower caper, a leafy jest,
Nature's pranks at their very best.

In this patch of mirth and cheer,
Every bud whispers, "Come, my dear!"
The soil breathes with laughter's tease,
Life's a canvas, painted with ease.

The Chorus of Sunlit Growth

Oh, they sway, the jolly greens,
Sharing all their silly scenes.
A tomato trips on its own vine,
Laughs aloud, "This is divine!"

Carrots peek from below the dirt,
Giggling hard, they are not hurt.
One says, "I'm not a veggie!
Check my top, I look quite edgy!"

The sun-drenched stage lights up the scene,
A dais of laughter, fresh and keen.
With cheeky roots dancing below,
Nature's concert, stealing the show.

Crickets chirp a funky beat,
As blooms and bugs all move their feet.
Life in shades of green and glee,
Join the chorus, wild and free!

Threads of Life and Literature

In a book where leaves entwine,
Stories crawl upon the spine.
Each page giggles with delight,
As ink spills secrets, day and night.

The author's pen begins to dance,
Characters twirl, given a chance.
A plot twist causes quite a stir,
While paper birds flap and purr.

With every chapter, vines emerge,
Boundless tales begin to surge.
A whimsical web of truth and jest,
Imagination's tour, a bold quest.

In this land of fiber and threads,
The stories laugh where reason treads.
Life's a tapestry, fun to weave,
Join the yarns, stay and believe!

A Tangle of Whispered Dreams

In a meadow where wishes grow,
A dreamer trips, and there they go.
The grass whispers, "Careful now,
Those daisies know just when to bow!"

Clouds cuddle, offering a grin,
As dragons dance with a silly spin.
The butterflies joke, fluttering near,
"Don't be shy, we're glad you're here!"

A wish would flutter, tumble down,
Tickled by laughter, not a frown.
In this mess of dreams and schemes,
Reality winks, bursting seams.

So join the fuss, the tangled spree,
Where laughter blooms like wild parsley.
In this patch of fanciful whims,
Life's a giggle; indulge in grins.

The Dance of the Wild

In the woods where critters prance,
A squirrel tries to lead a dance.
The rabbit hops, but slips, oh dear!
The raccoon munches, no time for cheer.

The fox watches with a snicker,
While the owl hoots, it grows much thicker.
A deer joins in but trips on a log,
And all burst out laughing—what a fog!

With twirls and spins, a laughter riot,
Each one thinks they're the true diet.
As moonlight gleams and shadows dart,
They sway like fools, but bless their heart!

So if you're lost in nature's glee,
Just follow the sounds and you might see:
A wild party 'neath the starry veil,
Where the fool's in fur will always prevail.

Serenade of the Forest

A tree sings low, a branch so high,
While crickets chirp a lullaby.
The fox is off, chasing his tail,
With a curious cat watching, pale.

The raccoons perform with pots and pans,
Like furry little rockstar bands.
A chatterbox parrot starts to squawk,
Drawing in all for a funny talk.

Bamboo flutes in the cool night air,
A bard of bad jokes, but folks don't care.
They laugh and cheer for the nonsense spree,
In the forest where smiles grow free!

With every screech and every sigh,
A chorus of giggles fills the sky.
Under moonlit glow, they prance and sway,
In harmony, they'll dance 'til break of day.

Roots Beneath the Surface

Below the ground where secrets lurk,
There's a party where the worms all smirk.
They wriggle and laugh, a wormy bunch,
Dancing on soil, oh what a crunch!

The moles dig deep and deliver the jokes,
While ants march in, amused little folks.
A radish tries to join but gets stuck,
Oh my, the roots just ran out of luck!

The beetles beetle in with shiny shells,
While a gopher spins tales of sugarcane bells.
A funnier tale has never been told,
Of roots that sway as the night unfolds.

So listen closely to the ground's soft hum,
Where laughter echoes, and giggles come.
For beneath our feet, the fun never dims,
As it tickles the earth and sings sweet hymns.

Lush Imagery at Dusk

At dusk, a canvas painted bright,
With hues and giggles in pure sight.
The flowers dance, they shake and sway,
As bees buzz past and jokingly play.

The sun dips down, and shadows sprout,
A hedgehog rolls, oh, what a spout!
He claims he's smooth, a suave old chap,
But on the grass, he takes a nap.

The brook chuckles with every splash,
While frogs croak secrets in a flash.
A butterfly twirls, wearing flair,
Turns out, it's lost!—beyond repair.

So gather 'round in the twilight glow,
Where laughter lingers, the warmth will flow.
In vibrant hues, as daylight fades,
Nature chuckles, as joy cascades.

Serenade of the Forest Floor

In the shade where whispers play,
Bugs perform a waltzy sway,
The mushrooms dance in little shoes,
As squirrels share their nutty blues.

With leaves that tickle every toe,
And shadows casting quite the show,
The ants march on with tiny drums,
While nature laughs and softly hums.

A rabbit sings a high-pitched tune,
While crickets join beneath the moon,
The forest floor is quite the stage,
As laughter leaps from page to page.

So if you're feeling down and low,
Just drop by where the wild things grow,
For every root and every sprout,
Has a story worth a playful shout.

Woven Wishes

In tangled threads of daytime dreams,
Where sunlight splits in silly beams,
The dandelions blow their seeds,
And giggle at our silly deeds.

The petals flounce in breezy jest,
While bees debate who's dressed the best,
A jumping bean joins in the fun,
While spiders weave a web to run.

The grasshoppers boast of long-lost bets,
As ladybugs tell silly threats,
With each new wish the laughter grows,
Like ticklish grass beneath our toes.

So if you wander through this place,
With cheeky winds that tease your face,
Just know that joy is woven tight,
In every wish that takes to flight.

Lattice of Lost Verses

In tangled lines where laughter hides,
The bumbled words take silly rides,
A ladybug drafts a ballad quick,
While lizards join in with a flick.

The rusty gate sings tales of old,
Of treasures that are under sold,
A squirrel spins yarns of nuts and glee,
As secrets slip through every tree.

The chatter of the leaves so bright,
Gives poets pause in pure delight,
With quips and jests that flutter down,
To make a jester of the town.

So if you find the verses lost,
Just pay attention to the cost,
For laughter in the wild prevails,
In every twist, the humor sails.

The Chime of Thickets

In thickets thick with giggling sprigs,
Where shadows wear their leafy wigs,
The wind whistles a funky tune,
As trees canoodle beneath the moon.

A poppy sways, a shy debut,
While daisies dance, a rolling crew,
The twilight sparkles, bursts with light,
As frogs take center stage tonight.

With every ripple on the stream,
Nature pours her playful dream,
And echoes sound with joyful zest,
In thickets where the heart feels blessed.

So join the mirth, let laughter soar,
In nature's show we all explore,
For in the thicket's joyful chime,
Lies all the magic of our time.

Entwined Dreams

In a garden where giggles grow,
Plants weave tales in breezes' blow.
The cucumbers plot a grand escape,
While carrots dance in a musty cape.

A tomato wears a charming hat,
While radishes sing a cheeky chat.
The peas joke about their tall estate,
And onions cry with laughter innate.

Bees buzz tunes of sweet delight,
As flowers wink, all dressed up bright.
The sun gives rise to a daring plot,
Where every leaf knows just what's hot.

In this haven, the laughter combines,
With roots and shoots forming funny lines.
Each bloom inspires a joyful chime,
In this patch where silliness is prime.

Cadence of Climbing Shadows

In a jungle of jests and playful sprout,
The quirky liana decided to shout.
It tangled with trees, entwined with a grin,
Whispering secrets from thick to thin.

A lizard danced on a winding spree,
Making moves like it owned the tree.
The shadows giggled, a playful sight,
While the sun pointed fingers, wanting a bite.

With every twist, a tale came to light,
Climbing high, avoiding the fright.
A monkey chortled, swinging away,
As shadows contorted in a bright ballet.

In this tango of life, the mischief flows,
Just nature's pranksters, striking a pose.
Each creak and rustle a grand little play,
As dusk settles down, they frolic away.

The Language of Leaves

Leaves flutter like whispers in the air,
Chirping secrets without a care.
The oak insists it's wise by heart,
While the willow rolls its eyes in art.

The maple brags its colors are bold,
While the grass giggles at tales of old.
A fern fans itself, feeling quite grand,
As petals clamor to make a stand.

In this leafy realm, humor ignites,
Each rustling branch shares quirky sights.
The roots chuckle; they know the score,
While the soil listens, wanting more.

Through seasons changing, the jokes do thrive,
As nature's chorus keeps spirits alive.
With every breeze, laughter takes flight,
In the greenery's jam, everything feels right.

Interlaced Stanzas

Words entwined like a playful twist,
Each thought a petal that can't be missed.
Sentences climb like a cheeky vine,
As phrases hop-scotch, feeling divine.

A pun's a seed that sprouts with glee,
While jokes take root under the tree.
Metaphors dance in soft sunlight,
And similes giggle, feeling just right.

Each stanza juggles rhymes with flair,
As quips and quarks float through the air.
The rhythm prances, a silly sight,
As laughter blossoms, pure delight.

In this garden of whimsical verse,
Story and humor break the curse.
With each line written, let joy arise,
In interlaced stanzas, the heart complies.

www.ingramcontent.com/pod-product-compliance
Lightning Source LLC
Chambersburg PA
CBHW072132070526
44585CB00016B/1637